Easter Cooking
and other fun stuff for Kids

Fiona Hammond

The Five Mile Press

The Five Mile Press
1 Centre Road, Scoresby
Victoria 3179 Australia
www.fivemile.com.au

Recipes and styling: Fiona Hammond
Internal design: Anne-Marie Reeves
Photography: Greg Elms Photography
Illustrations: Karen Carter
Recipe editor: Rachel Pitts
A CIP record is available from the
National Library Australia
First published 2011
Printed in China 5 4 3 2 1

Contents

Bunny down a burrow ice-creams   4

Butterfly pastries   6

Carrot cakes   8

Bunny mask   10

Chocolate brownie ice-cream sandwiches   12

Sugar-and-spice chocolate rabbits   14

White chocolate truffle hens   16

Carrot paper cone   18

Daffodil custard tarts   20

Dried-fruit balls   22

Dyed eggs   24

Cinnamon toast flowers   26

Greek orange biscuits   28

Egg-carton daffodils   30

Hot cross muffins   32

Speckled meringue nests   34

Egg card   36

Poppy chocolate tarts   38

Rocky road hedgehog   40

Spinach and ricotta filo nest pies   42

Pompom chick   44

 = adult supervision required

Bunny down a burrow ice-creams

Makes 6 ice-creams

INGREDIENTS

100 g (3½ oz) milk chocolate, broken

¼ cup green sprinkles

6 ice-cream cones with a flat base

chocolate ice-cream to scoop

6 pink marshmallows

3 white mini marshmallows

EQUIPMENT

small heatproof bowl

small saucepan

metal spoon

shallow bowl

ice-cream scoop

scissors

toothpick

1

Place the chocolate in a small heatproof bowl. Set the bowl over a small saucepan of gently simmering water, making sure the bowl doesn't touch the water. Stir until the chocolate melts then remove from the heat. Cool to room temperature.

2

Put the green sprinkles in a shallow bowl.

3

Dip the top edge of an ice-cream cone into the melted chocolate to a depth of about 1 cm ($\frac{2}{5}$ in). Allow excess chocolate to drip off.

4

Dip the cone into the green sprinkles, sticking some to the chocolate – this is the grass around the burrow.

5

Repeat steps 3 and 4 with the remaining ice-cream cones, then place them in the refrigerator for 5 minutes to set the chocolate.

6

Place a scoop of ice-cream in each cone and place the cones in the freezer for 10-15 minutes to set the ice-cream firmly in place.

TIP
You can freeze the ice-cream cones for up to 2 hours before adding the marshmallows. If you want to store them for longer, place them in an airtight container or in individual cellophane bags.

7

Use scissors to cut each pink marshmallow in half horizontally. These will be the bunnies' paws. Place them cut-side down on a work surface. Dip the end of a toothpick into the remaining melted chocolate and, using it like a paintbrush, place 3 drops at one end of each marshmallow, for the toes. Leave the toes to set.

8

Dip the cut side of 2 marshmallow paws into the remaining melted chocolate and stick them onto one side of an ice-cream top about 1 cm ($\frac{2}{5}$ in) apart, with the toes sticking out. Repeat with each ice-cream top.

9

Cut each mini marshmallow in half horizontally. Dip the halves cut-side down into the melted chocolate and stick them in the middle of the ice-cream tops, for the tails.

Butterfly pastries

Makes 20 pastries

INGREDIENTS
¼ cup (55 g/2 oz) caster (superfine) sugar
1 frozen puff pastry sheet, thawed

EQUIPMENT
2 baking trays
baking paper
cook's knife
chopping board
wire rack

BEFORE YOU START
Line 2 baking trays with baking paper.

1
Sprinkle half of the sugar onto a work surface covering an area of about 25 x 25 cm (10 x 10 in).

2
Place the pastry sheet onto the sugar. Sprinkle the remaining sugar over the pastry.

3
Cut 2 strips of pastry about 5 mm (⅕ in) wide from one side of the pastry sheet. Set aside. Cut the pastry sheet in half to form 2 rectangles.

4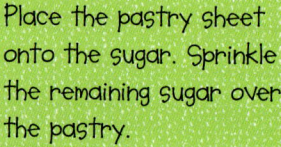
Roll up 1 of the rectangles starting from a long edge, stopping once you get to the centre. Roll up the other side to meet in the centre. Repeat with the other rectangle.

5
Transfer the pastry rolls and the long pastry strips to a baking tray and refrigerate for 20 minutes.

6

Preheat the oven to 160°C (320°F). Remove the tray from the refrigerator and transfer the pastry rolls to a chopping board. Cut each one into 20 slices of around 5 mm ($\frac{1}{5}$ in) in width, for the wings (you need 40 wings). Then cut each long strip into 10 lengths of about 1.5 cm ($\frac{3}{5}$ in), for the bodies (you need 20 bodies).

7

To make a butterfly, lay 2 wings next to each other on a tray with the flat sides of the wings touching. Place a body in the centre of the wings. Continue making butterflies with the remaining wings and bodies, and arrange the butterflies about 2 cm ($\frac{4}{5}$ in) apart on the trays.

8

Bake in the oven for 15-18 minutes or until golden and crisp. Leave to rest for 3 minutes then carefully transfer to a wire rack to cool.

Carrot cakes

Makes 12 cakes

INGREDIENTS

Cake

1 cup (185 g/6½ oz) brown sugar

2 eggs

¾ cup (185 ml/6½ fl oz) sunflower oil

1½ cups (225 g/8 oz) wholemeal self-raising flour

1 teaspoon bicarbonate of soda

1 teaspoon ground cinnamon

2 cups coarsely grated carrot

Topping

1½ cups (180 g/6½ oz) icing (confectioners') sugar

1 tablespoon orange juice

1 tablespoon warm water

50 g (2 oz) plain chocolate biscuits

6 plump whole dried apricots

6 mint leaf candies

EQUIPMENT

12-hole muffin tray

12 paper cupcake cases

large and small mixing bowls

whisk

sieve

wooden spoon

skewer

wire rack

spatula

plastic zip-lock bag

rolling pin

shallow bowl

small sharp knife

BEFORE YOU START

Line the holes of the muffin tray with paper cases. Preheat the oven to 180°C (350°F).

Place the sugar, eggs and oil in a large mixing bowl and whisk together to mix well.

Sift the flour, bicarbonate of soda and cinnamon into the bowl. You may find some husks from the wholemeal flour left in the sieve – add these to the bowl. Stir with a wooden spoon to combine well.

Stir in the carrot until well combined.

4

Spoon the cake mixture evenly into the cupcake cases.

5

Bake in the oven for 20-25 minutes, or until a skewer comes out clean when inserted into a cake. Transfer the cakes to a wire rack to cool completely.

6

To decorate the cakes, sift the icing sugar into a small mixing bowl. Stir in the orange juice and enough warm water to make a smooth, thick icing (you may not need all of the water). Spread a thin layer of icing over the top of each cooled cake.

7

Place the biscuits in a zip-lock bag and bash with a rolling pin to form chocolate 'soil'. Tip into a shallow bowl. Dip the iced top of the cakes into the soil.

8

Cut the dried apricots into mini carrot shapes. Using the tip of the knife, make an incision in the top of each apricot 'carrot' and add a piece of mint leaf to the incision, for the leaves.

9

Gently press a carrot into the top of each cake.

Bunny mask

EQUIPMENT
pencil
tracing paper
A4 sheet of pale pink or
brown card
scissors
fabric scraps for nose
and ears
glue
wool for whiskers
sticky tape or stapler
hole-puncher
30 cm (12 in) hat elastic

1

Trace the bunny mask template on page 48 onto tracing paper, including the nose and ears. Place the tracing paper over the coloured card and slowly redraw around the mask (but not the nose or ears), pressing down to transfer onto the card. Cut out the mask from the card. Cut out the holes for the eyes. Mark the dotted line beneath the nose on the back of the mask.

2

Cut out the nose and ears from the tracing paper.

3

Cut out the nose and ears from your selected fabrics by holding the tracing paper shapes against the fabrics and cutting around them. Glue the ears onto the mask.

4

Cut wool strands for the whiskers. Glue whiskers into place then glue the nose over the top.

When the glue has dried, cut along the dotted line under the nose. Overlap the cut edges by about 1.5 cm ($\frac{3}{5}$ in) and secure them in place with sticky tape along the back of the mask, or with staples.

Punch holes about 1 cm ($\frac{2}{5}$ in) in from the sides of the mask. Tie elastic between the holes, adjusting the length to suit your head (you might need someone to help with this).

Chocolate brownie ice-cream sandwiches

Makes 6 sandwiches

Ingredients

125 g (4 oz) unsalted butter, plus extra for greasing tin
150 g (5 oz) dark chocolate, roughly chopped
⅔ cup (125 g/4 oz) brown sugar
3 eggs
¾ cup (110 g/3½ oz) plain (all-purpose) flour
150 g (5 oz) milk or white chocolate, roughly chopped
vanilla or chocolate ice-cream to scoop
icing (confectioners') sugar to dust

Equipment

pencil
baking paper
scissors
square 20 x 20 cm (8 x 8 in) cake tin
heatproof mixing bowl
saucepan
metal spoon
whisk
sieve
wooden spoon
skewer
small sharp knife

Before you start

1. Trace the paper egg and zigzag template on page 47 onto baking paper. Cut out the egg zigzag shape.
2. Preheat the oven to 180°C (350°F).

1

Rub the cake tin with a little butter. Cut 2 pieces of baking paper 20 cm (8 in) wide and 35 cm (14 in) long. Stick a piece into the tin covering the base and going up two of the sides. Stick in the other piece, covering the remaining sides and overlapping the base.

2

Place the butter and dark chocolate in a heatproof mixing bowl. Set the bowl over a saucepan of gently simmering water, making sure the bowl doesn't touch the water. Stir until the chocolate and butter melt then remove from the heat. Cool to lukewarm.

3

Whisk the sugar and eggs into the chocolate mixture until well combined.

4

Sift the flour onto the mixture and use a wooden spoon to stir until just combined. Stir in the pieces of milk or white chocolate.

5

Pour the mixture into the cake tin. Bake in the oven for 25 minutes, or until a skewer comes out with moist crumbs on it. Leave to cool in the tin.

6

Remove the brownie cake from the tin. Cut 6 egg shapes from the cake by cutting around the paper egg. Slice each egg in half horizontally.

7

Cut out 6 zigzag strips. This will be used to make a decorative icing-sugar pattern on top of the sandwiches after you add the ice-cream.

8

Now get someone to help you work quickly so that the ice-cream doesn't melt. Open out each brownie sandwich and place a spoon of ice-cream on the bottom piece, then cover with the top piece and press to flatten slightly.

9

Lay the zigzag strip across the centre of a brownie sandwich and sift icing sugar over the top. Remove the strip to reveal pattern. Repeat with remaining sandwiches. Serve straight away.

Tip
You can prepare these sandwiches in advance and store them in the freezer. Decorate with icing sugar once you take them out of the freezer, and allow them to thaw a little so the brownie is not too cold and hard.

Sugar-and-spice chocolate rabbits

Makes 20 rabbits

Ingredients

100 g (3½ oz) unsalted butter, softened
¼ cup (55 g/2 oz) caster (superfine) sugar
2 teaspoons milk
1 cup (150 g/5 oz) plain (all-purpose) flour,
  plus extra to dust
¼ cup (30 g/1 oz) cocoa powder
½ teaspoon baking powder
1 teaspoon ground cinnamon
2 tablespoons raw sugar

Equipment

2 baking trays
baking paper
mixing bowl
electric beaters
sieve
plastic wrap
rolling pin
6 cm (2½ in) rabbit-shaped
  biscuit cutter

Before you start

Line 2 baking trays with baking paper.

1 Put the butter and caster sugar in a mixing bowl and beat with electric beaters until pale and creamy. Add the milk and beat to mix well.

2 Sift the flour, cocoa, baking powder and cinnamon onto the butter mixture.

3 Use your hands to mix the ingredients together to form a dough. Shape into a ball and then flatten it into a disc about 1 cm (⅖ in) thick. Cover with plastic wrap and refrigerate for 20 minutes.

Tip
You can giftwrap biscuits in clear cellophane bags and tie with egg cards (see page 36 and 37).

4

Preheat the oven to 180°C (350°F). Dust a work surface and rolling pin with some flour. Roll the chilled dough out to 5 mm ($\frac{1}{5}$ in) thick. Cut into rabbit shapes with the biscuit cutter and transfer the rabbits to baking trays. Gather the dough off-cuts and roll into another ball. Re-roll the dough to 5 mm ($\frac{1}{5}$ in) thick and cut out more rabbits.

5

Sprinkle the raw sugar over the top of the rabbits.

6

Bake the rabbits in the oven for 10 minutes. Remove the tray from the oven and leave the rabbits to cool completely on the trays. Store in an airtight container for up to 1 week.

White chocolate truffle hens

Makes 16 hens

INGREDIENTS

250 g (9 oz) white chocolate,
  roughly chopped, plus 50 g
  (2 oz) coarsely grated
½ cup (125 ml/4 fl oz) cream
8 raspberry candies
small length of red licorice lace
16 yellow mini sugar-coated
  chocolates such as mini M&Ms

EQUIPMENT

small heatproof bowl
small saucepan
metal spoon
shallow bowl
tray or plate
baking paper
teaspoon
small sharp knife
scissors
16 coloured mini paper
  cupcake cases

1

Place the broken chocolate and cream in a small heatproof bowl. Set the bowl over a small saucepan of gently simmering water, making sure the bowl doesn't touch the water. Stir until the chocolate melts.

2

Remove the bowl from the heat and place in the refrigerator. Leave to chill for 2 hours until the mixture is just set.

3

Put the grated chocolate in a shallow bowl or saucer. Line a tray or plate with baking paper.

4

Take 16 heaped teaspoons of the mixture and roll into balls.

5

Roll the balls in grated chocolate. Transfer the balls to the tray or plate.

6

Cut 2 thin slices from the centre of each raspberry candy. Press a slice on top of each ball, for the hen's comb.

7

Use scissors to cut 32 small pieces of red licorice lace for the eyes. Press 2 pieces on each ball beneath the comb.

TIP
If the chocolate truffle balls become too soft while decorating, chill them in the refrigerator until firm enough to handle.

8

Press a yellow sugar-coated chocolate below the eyes, for the beak.

9

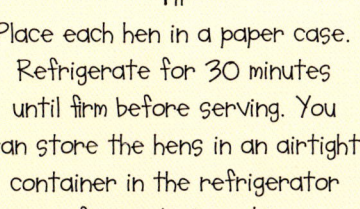

TIP
Place each hen in a paper case. Refrigerate for 30 minutes until firm before serving. You can store the hens in an airtight container in the refrigerator for up to 1 week.

Carrot paper cone

EQUIPMENT

A4 sheet of orange paper
ruler
pencil
green paper serviette, about
20 x 20 cm (8 x 8 in)

1

Lay the sheet of paper horizontally on a work surface (one of the long edges should be closest to you).

2

Use a ruler and a pencil to make some marks 5 cm (2 in) in from the left short edge. Fold the paper in at the marks to make a light crease (A), then open the paper out flat again.

3

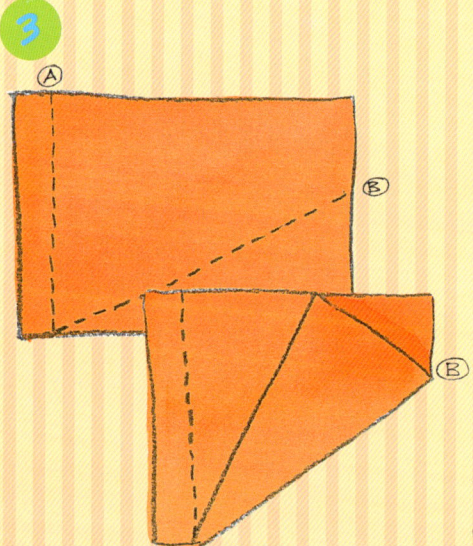

Put your left index finger on the left side of the crease at the bottom of the paper. Use your right hand to pick up the bottom right corner and fold it up to the top of the paper. This fold should make a shape like a large carrot with a pointy tip. Press down on the fold to make a light crease. (B)

4

Fold the pointy carrot over again taking it to your first crease line.

5

Wrap the left flap around the carrot. Fold up the pointy tip of the carrot so the paper stays in place.

6

Gently push your hand into the top of the carrot to open it into a cone. Set it aside while you make the leaves with the serviette.

7

Pinch the folded corner of the serviette with one hand. Slide your other hand into the middle of the serviette and ruffle it open so it looks like some floppy leaves.

8

Insert the pinched corner of the serviette into the carrot and ruffle up the leaves.

Tip
Hand out these carrot cones for an Easter egg hunt. They are great for collecting lots of mini eggs!

Daffodil custard tarts

Makes 12 tarts

INGREDIENTS

2 frozen shortcrust pastry sheets, thawed,
   or pre-baked shortcrust tart cases
1 egg
1 egg yolk (see Tip for how to separate eggs)
½ teaspoon vanilla essence
⅔ cup (165 ml/6 fl oz) milk
⅔ cup (165 ml/6 fl oz) cream
¼ cup (55 g/2 oz) caster (superfine) sugar
ground nutmeg to sprinkle

EQUIPMENT

pencil
tracing or baking paper
scissors
yellow or orange card
6 cm (2½ in) round biscuit cutter
12-hole non-stick mini muffin tray
whisk
mixing bowl
small saucepan
sieve
jug

BEFORE YOU START

1. Trace the daffodil template on page 46 onto tracing or baking paper. Place the tracing paper over coloured card and slowly redraw around the daffodil, pressing down to transfer onto the card. Trace out another 11 daffodils, then cut them out of the card.
2. Preheat the oven to 160°C (320°F).

1

Cut out 12 rounds of the pastry with a 6 cm (2½ in) biscuit cutter.

2

Line the muffin holes with the pastry rounds, gently pressing them into the base and sides of the holes. The pastry should come over the top of the holes, so you can press the extra pastry over the edge to look like a rim of petals. Refrigerate for 20 minutes.

3

Meanwhile, start the custard by whisking the whole egg, the egg yolk and vanilla in a bowl.

4

Heat the milk and cream in a small saucepan over medium heat until just warm, being careful it doesn't boil. Remove from the heat and stir in the sugar until dissolved.

5

Pour the warm liquid over the egg mixture, whisking gently until combined.

6

Pour the mixture through a sieve into a jug to remove any large egg particles.

7

Bake the chilled pastry cases in the oven for 8 minutes. Carefully remove them from the oven and pour the custard mixture into the cases.

8

Bake for another 20 minutes or until the custard sets. To test, lightly touch the middle of a tart – it should feel firm. Sprinkle the tarts with nutmeg and leave to cool.

9

Place each tart in the centre of a paper daffodil.

To serve, place each tart in the centre of a paper daffodil.

TIP

To separate the egg, get 2 bowls ready. Crack the egg, then hold it in one hand and gently open it with your thumb. Tip the egg into the cupped palm of your other hand, holding your hand above a bowl. Open your fingers slightly and allow the white to slip through into the bowl. Drop the yolk into the other bowl.

Dried-fruit balls

Makes 16 balls

INGREDIENTS

1 cup (180 g/6½ oz) dried apricots

1 cup (130 g/4 oz) dried cranberries

¼ cup (25 g/1 oz) desiccated coconut

2 tablespoons orange juice

⅓ cup multicoloured sprinkles

EQUIPMENT

food processor

teaspoon

shallow bowl

plate

serving bowl or mini paper cupcake cases

TIP
If not eating the balls on the same day, prepare them up to step 3, store in the refrigerator and roll in sprinkles just before serving.

1

Place the apricots, cranberries and coconut in a food processor and blend until finely chopped.

2

Add the orange juice and blend until well combined.

3

Take heaped teaspoons of the mixture and roll into balls.

4

Place the sprinkles in a shallow bowl. Roll the balls in sprinkles, coating them evenly, and place on a plate. Refrigerate for 1 hour until firm.

5

To serve, arrange the balls in a bowl or in mini paper cupcake cases. You can store the balls in an airtight container in the refrigerator for up to 2 weeks.

TIP
For gifts, wrap the fruit balls in squares of cellophane tied with ribbon at the top.

Dyed eggs

Equipment

6 eggs

saucepan

water

spoon

bowl

assorted food colouring

glass

vinegar

newspaper

straw

wire rack

1

Place the eggs in a saucepan and cover with water. Bring to the boil, then reduce the heat to a simmer. Simmer for 7 minutes, then carefully spoon the eggs into a bowl of cold water. Leave to cool completely.

2

Put 2 teaspoons of the food colouring of your choice into a glass. Add 1 tablespoon of vinegar and enough cold water to three-quarter fill the glass.

3

Immerse an egg into the coloured water using the spoon. Leave for 3 minutes or until coloured to your liking, then remove from water.

4

Place the egg on a work surface covered in newspaper. Place a drop of different colouring on the egg.

5

Blow hard through a straw onto the dye to disperse it over the egg and create interesting patterns.

6

Transfer the egg to a wire rack to dry while you dye the remaining eggs.

The hardboiled eggs will keep in the refrigerator for up to 4 days.

HISTORY OF THE EASTER EGG

Easter is the Christian celebration of the rising of Christ on Easter Sunday. In the Northern Hemisphere Easter falls during springtime, a time of regrowth and birth after the long cold winter. Easter eggs are the main symbol of Easter because the egg represents a new life and has become a symbol of Christ's resurrection.

The giving of eggs at Easter is popular around the world. Various cultures have developed traditions over the centuries where hen or duck eggs are beautifully decorated and coloured. Originally, natural vegetable dyes were used. In Greece, whole hard-boiled eggs are dyed red to represent the blood of Christ. 'Pysanky' is the name given to decorated Ukrainian Easter eggs. A special stylus is used to draw the patterns with wax onto the egg shell. The egg is then dyed and the process is repeated in multiple layers of wax and colours. Finally the wax is melted away to reveal an intricate and colourful pattern. Eggs are also hand-blown to empty the inside contents, then painted with detailed patterns and images, or splendidly decorated with jewels. These blown eggs can be kept forever.

Today chocolate eggs are the popular alternative to give at Easter, but many cultures still dye and decorate eggs to present to friends and loved ones with Easter greetings. Here is a fun way to dye your own Easter eggs for friends and family – don't forget you can eat them (if kept refrigerated).

Cinnamon toast flowers

Makes 12 flowers (3 per person)

INGREDIENTS

3 eggs
2 tablespoons milk
½ teaspoon ground cinnamon
12 slices of square bread, a day
 or more old
1 tablespoon butter
icing (confectioners') sugar
 to dust
maple syrup to drizzle

EQUIPMENT

mixing bowl
whisk
large flower-shaped biscuit
 cutter
large non-stick frying pan
egglifter
plate

TIP
Bread dipped in beaten egg and fried is called 'French toast' and is a great way of using up older bread.

1

Put the eggs, milk and cinnamon in a mixing bowl and whisk to combine well.

2

Use a large flower-shaped biscuit cutter to cut a flower from each slice of bread.

3

Heat a large non-stick frying pan over medium heat. Melt half of the butter in the pan and use an egglifter to spread it evenly over the base.

4

Dip a bread flower in the egg mixture, coating each side. Hold it above the bowl to drain off excess egg and place it in the frying pan. Quickly repeat with 5 more flowers, adding all to the pan to cook at the same time.

5

Cook the flowers for 2 minutes, until golden brown, then turn them with the egglifter and cook for another 1–2 minutes on the other side. Lift onto a plate and repeat steps 3, 4 and 5 with the remaining butter and flowers.

6 Serve the hot toast flowers dusted with icing sugar and drizzled with maple syrup. You may also like to scatter with fresh strawberries or blueberries.

Tip
If you don't have a flower-shaped biscuit cutter, you can use the poppy template on page 47. Trace it onto tracing or baking paper and cut out the template. Hold it against the bread and cut around it with scissors.

Greek orange biscuits

Makes 30 biscuits

INGREDIENTS

1 orange
½ cup (110 g/3½ oz) caster (superfine) sugar
90 g (3 oz) unsalted butter, softened
1 egg
1½ cups (225 g/8 oz) plain (all-purpose) flour
½ teaspoon baking powder
1 cup (120 g/4 oz) icing (confectioners') sugar

EQUIPMENT

3 baking trays
baking paper
box grater
mixing bowl
electric beaters
sieve
wooden spoon

BEFORE YOU START

Line 2 of the baking trays with baking paper. Preheat the oven to 180°C (350°F).

Grate the zest of the orange using the fine side of a box grater, taking a thin layer of skin without too much of the white pith underneath.

Put the sugar and butter in a mixing bowl and beat with electric beaters until pale and creamy.

Add the orange zest and egg and beat together.

Sift the flour and baking powder onto the butter mixture. Stir with a wooden spoon until well combined.

Divide the dough into 30 even pieces. Use your hands to roll a piece into a log 8 cm (3 in) long. Transfer to a tray lined with paper and shape into a horseshoe, a round or 'S' shape, even an '8' shape. Repeat with the remaining pieces of dough, filling up the 2 trays.

6

Bake the biscuits in the oven for 10 minutes or until firm but only lightly golden. Leave to cool on the trays for 2 minutes.

7

Sift half of the icing sugar onto a clean tray. Place the warm biscuits on the icing sugar. Sift the remaining icing sugar over the biscuits and leave to cool completely. Take the biscuits out of the icing sugar (some icing sugar should be stuck to the surface of the biscuits) and store in an airtight container for up to 1 week.

Egg-carton daffodils

1

Cut out the individual cups from the egg carton – these will be the outer rim of the daffodil flowers. Neatly trim the cup edges.

2

Cut out the dividing sections in between the cups – when you turn them upside down they become tall, thin cups, and these are the middles of the flowers. Neatly trim the cup edges.

3

Paint the larger cups with red paint. Paint the smaller cups orange. Allow to dry.

4

Pierce the base of each small and large cup with the point of the scissors.

5

To make the daffodils, thread a green pipe-cleaner through a large red cup and then through a small orange cup. Slide the cups to the top of the pipe-cleaner with the small cup sitting inside the large cup. Fold over the top of the pipe-cleaner and twist the strands together to hold it in place and to form the stamen of the flower.

TIP
Tie a ribbon around a bunch of daffodils to give as an Easter gift, or place in a narrow vase to decorate your Easter table. Or, tie a daffodil to a bag of edible goodies by winding the pipe-cleaner around the top of the bag.

Hot cross muffins

Makes 12 muffins

INGREDIENTS

Muffins

1 orange

125 g (4 oz) unsalted butter

2 cups (300 g/10½ oz) self-raising flour

2 teaspoons ground cinnamon

½ teaspoon mixed spice

½ cup (110 g/3½ oz) caster (superfine) sugar

2 eggs

¾ cup (185 ml/6½ fl oz) milk

1 cup (150 g/5 oz) currants

½ cup (90 g/3 oz) chopped dried apricots (optional)

Icing

½ cup (60 g/2 oz) icing (confectioners') sugar

2 teaspoons orange juice

1 teaspoon warm water

EQUIPMENT

12-hole muffin tray

12 paper cupcake cases

box grater

citrus juicer

small saucepan

sieve

mixing bowls

wooden spoon

whisk

skewer

wire rack

plastic zip-lock bag

scissors

BEFORE YOU START

Line the muffin holes with paper cases. Preheat the oven to 180°C (350°F).

1

Grate the orange zest using the fine side of a box grater, taking a thin layer of skin without white pith underneath. Then juice the orange.

2

Melt the butter in a small saucepan over medium heat. Remove from the heat and leave to cool to lukewarm.

3

Sift the flour, cinnamon and mixed spice into a large mixing bowl. Stir in the sugar with a wooden spoon.

4

In a medium mixing bowl, whisk together the melted butter, eggs, milk, orange zest and 2 tablespoons of orange juice.

5

Add the egg mixture to the bowl of flour, sugar and spices and stir until just combined. Gently stir in the dried fruit.

6

Spoon the mixture into the muffin cases. Bake in the oven for 20 minutes or until a skewer comes out clean when inserted into a muffin. Transfer to a wire rack to cool completely.

7

To make the icing, sift the icing sugar into a small mixing bowl. Stir in the orange juice and warm water to make a smooth, thick icing.

8

Spoon the icing into a zip-lock bag and seal shut. Use scissors to snip a very small hole in a corner of the bag so you can use the bag for piping. Gently squeeze the icing towards the hole and slowly pipe a cross on top of each muffin.

TIP
For the best muffins, stir the batter until just combined, leaving it slightly lumpy. Don't be tempted to mix to a smoother batter as too much mixing results in rubbery muffins.

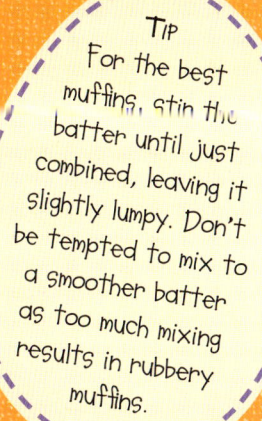

TIP
You can also make chocolate icing for the cross by adding 1 tablespoon of cocoa powder and 3–4 teaspoons of milk to the icing sugar to form a thick paste.

Speckled meringue nests

Makes 10 nests

INGREDIENTS

2 very fresh egg whites at room
   temperature (see Tip for how
   to separate eggs on page 21)
½ cup (110 g/3½ oz) caster
   (superfine) sugar
25 g (1 oz) dark chocolate,
   coarsely grated
mini chocolate Easter eggs to
   fill nests

EQUIPMENT

2 baking trays
baking paper
mixing bowl
electric beaters
spatula
metal spoon
wooden spoon

BEFORE YOU START

Line 2 baking trays with baking
paper. Preheat the oven to
120°C (250°F).

TIP
For an Easter dessert,
place a spoonful of whipped
cream into the hollow of
the nests and top with
fresh berries.

Put the egg whites in a clean,
dry mixing bowl and beat with
electric beaters until soft
peaks begin to form.

With the beaters still going,
gradually add the sugar a
spoonful at a time. Beat until
the mixture is glossy and
thick. Turn off the beaters
and lift them out of the
meringue mixture – the peaks
should hold firm.

Sprinkle the chocolate over
the mixture. Use a spatula to
stir the chocolate into the egg
whites as gently as possible.

Spoon 10 even mounds of
meringue onto the baking
trays, leaving 5 cm (2 in)
between each one to allow for
spreading.

TIP
For gifts,
wrap eggs in
nests in
squares of
cellophane and
tie with pompom
chicks
(see page 44).

5

Use the back of a metal spoon to hollow out the centre of each mound and create a nest shape. Move the spoon in one direction around the edge of each nest, dragging and lifting to create a few rough peaks.

6

Place the meringues in the oven and reduce the temperature to 100°C (210°F). Bake for 1½ hours, then turn the oven off and leave the door slightly open for the meringues to cool completely. (You can place the handle of a wooden spoon in the door opening.)

7

To serve, place Easter eggs in the meringue nests. The meringues can be stored in an airtight container for up to 1 week.

Egg card

EQUIPMENT
pencil
tracing paper
coloured card
scissors
selection of ribbon
glue
hole-puncher

1

Trace the egg on page 46 onto tracing paper. Place the tracing paper over the coloured card and slowly redraw around the egg, pressing down to transfer onto the card. Cut out the egg from the card.

2

Choose decorative ribbon to run across the middle of the egg and cut 7 cm (3 in) in length. Glue the ribbon to the egg and leave to dry.

3

Punch a hole in the top of the card. Cut a 20-30 cm (8-12 in) strand of thin ribbon and double it over. Insert the folded end into the hole and thread the loose strands through the loop. Pull to tighten the ribbon. Use this ribbon to attach the card to a gift.

1

Follow the instructions on the opposite page to cut out 2 eggs and remember to mark the cutting line on the template at the back of the eggs.

3D egg card

Equipment
pencil
tracing paper
2 sheets of card in contrasting colours
scissors
hole-puncher
thin ribbon

2

Cut along the lines on each egg. Slide 1 egg into the other and position them so the sides stick out from each other to create 4 even quarters when you look at the egg from above.

3

Follow step 3 on the opposite page to punch a hole in the top of the egg and attach ribbon.

Poppy chocolate tarts

Makes 12 tarts

INGREDIENTS

plain (all-purpose) flour to dust
1 quantity of Sugar-and-spice
   chocolate biscuit dough (page 14)
200 g (7 oz) milk chocolate
1 cup (250 ml/8½ fl oz) cream
50 g (2 oz) dark chocolate

BEFORE YOU START

1. Trace the poppy template on page 47 onto tracing or baking paper. Place the tracing paper over red card and slowly redraw around the poppy, pressing down to transfer onto the card. Trace out another 11 poppies, then cut them out of the card.

2. Preheat the oven to 180°C (350°F).

EQUIPMENT

pencil
tracing or baking paper
scissors
red card
rolling pin
6 cm (2½ in) round biscuit cutter
12-hole non-stick muffin tray
wire rack
small heatproof mixing bowl
small saucepan
metal spoon
tray or plate
toothpick

1

Dust a work surface and rolling pin with flour and roll out the biscuit dough to 5 mm (⅕ in) thick. Cut out 12 rounds with a 6 cm (2½ in) biscuit cutter.

2

Line the muffin holes with the rounds of dough, gently pressing them into the base and sides of the holes. Refrigerate for 20 minutes.

3

Bake the cases in the oven for 10 minutes. Leave to cool for 5 minutes then carefully remove from the muffin holes and place on a wire rack to cool completely.

4

To make the tart filling, place the milk chocolate in a small heatproof mixing bowl. Set aside.

5

Heat the cream in a small saucepan over medium heat until it just begins to boil.

6

Pour the hot cream over the chocolate and stir until the chocolate melts. Cool to room temperature.

7

Arrange the tart cases on a tray or plate and spoon the chocolate filling into each one. Refrigerate for 30 minutes or until set.

8

Place the dark chocolate in the cleaned heatproof bowl. Set the bowl over a small saucepan of gently simmering water, making sure the bowl doesn't touch the water. Stir until the chocolate melts then remove from the heat.

9

Dip the end of a toothpick into the melted chocolate and, using it like a paintbrush, paint small dots over the surface of each tart to resemble the centre of a poppy.

10

To serve, place each tart in the centre of a paper poppy.

Rocky road hedgehog

Makes 8 slices

INGREDIENTS

vegetable oil to grease the tin
1 cup (75 g/2½ oz) pink and
   white marshmallows
75 g (2½ oz) plain sweet biscuits
200 g (7 oz) milk or dark
   chocolate, broken
½ cup (30 g/1 oz) shredded
   coconut

EQUIPMENT

pastry brush
loaf tin (8 x 16 cm/3 x 6½ in)
baking paper
plastic zip-lock bag
rolling pin
heatproof mixing bowl
saucepan
metal spoon
cook's knife

1

Brush the loaf tin with a little vegetable oil. Cut a piece of baking paper to cover the base and long sides of the tin, then stick it into the tin. Cut another long, narrow piece to cover the ends and overlap the base.

2

Cut the marshmallows into quarters. Place the biscuits in a zip-lock bag and bash into chunks with a rolling pin.

3

Place the chocolate in a heatproof mixing bowl. Set the bowl over a saucepan of gently simmering water, making sure the bowl doesn't touch the water. Stir until the chocolate melts then remove from the heat. Cool until lukewarm.

4

Add the marshmallows, biscuits and coconut to the melted chocolate. Stir well with a metal spoon.

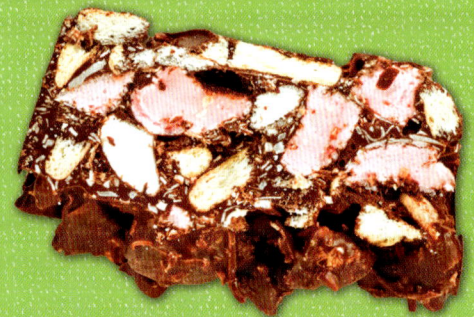

TIP
For gifts, wrap pieces of rocky road in rectangles of cellophane and tie the ends with ribbon.

5

Spoon the mixture into the loaf tin and spread evenly with the back of the spoon. Leave to set. This can take 1-4 hours depending on the weather – the cooler the temperature, the faster it sets.

6

Remove the rocky road from the tin and cut into 8 slices. Store in an airtight container for up to 2 weeks.

Spinach and ricotta filo nest pies

Makes 12 pies

INGREDIENTS

- 4 cups (200 g/7 oz) spinach leaves
- 2 tablespoons mint leaves
- 100 g (3½ oz) feta
- ½ cup (65 g/2 oz) frozen peas (optional)
- ¼ teaspoon freshly ground black pepper
- 300 g (10½ oz) ricotta
- 3 eggs
- 125 g (4 oz) unsalted butter, or ½ cup (125 ml/4 fl oz) olive oil
- 8 filo pastry sheets

EQUIPMENT

- colander
- tea towel
- cook's knife
- chopping board
- mixing bowls
- whisk
- wooden spoon
- small saucepan
- pastry brush
- 12-hole muffin tray

1

Wash the spinach leaves and drain them in a colander. Place on a clean tea towel and pat dry.

2

Finely chop the spinach and place it in a large mixing bowl. Chop the mint and add it to the bowl.

3

Use your hands to crumble the feta into the bowl. Add the peas (if using) and the pepper.

4

Put the ricotta and eggs in another mixing bowl and whisk together until smooth. Add to the spinach mixture and mix well with a wooden spoon.

5

Melt the butter in a small saucepan over medium heat. Brush some in the holes of the muffin tray. Preheat the oven to 180°C (350°F).

6

Spread the filo pastry on a work surface and cover with a damp tea towel to stop the filo from drying out.

7

Transfer 1 sheet of filo to another working area and brush with melted butter (or olive oil). Cover with another sheet of filo and brush with more butter. Repeat with 2 more sheets until you have 4 layers. Set the stack aside, and repeat this step with the remaining 4 sheets of filo. You should have 2 stacks.

8

Cut each filo stack into 6 even rectangles. Line each muffin hole with a rectangle of filo, pressing it into the base and sides. The filo should come up above the muffin holes.

9

Spoon the spinach mixture into the filo cases. Tuck in the overhanging filo to form a neat raised edge around each pie.

10

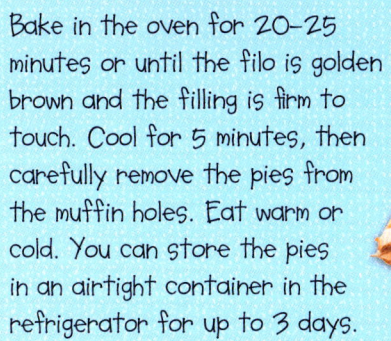

Bake in the oven for 20–25 minutes or until the filo is golden brown and the filling is firm to touch. Cool for 5 minutes, then carefully remove the pies from the muffin holes. Eat warm or cold. You can store the pies in an airtight container in the refrigerator for up to 3 days.

TIP
These pies also work with puff pastry. Cut 3 puff pastry sheets into 4 squares each and press them into the muffin holes without using butter. Fill with the spinach mixture and bake as in step 10.

Pompom chick

EQUIPMENT

pencil

tracing paper

cardboard (such as
from a cereal packet)

scissors

assorted coloured wool

large-eyed needle

scraps of red and black felt

plastic eyes

glue

1

Trace the ring template on page 46 onto tracing paper. Place the tracing paper over the card and slowly redraw around the ring, pressing down to transfer onto the card. Trace another ring onto the card, then cut out both rings.

2

Cut 3 x 2 m (6½ ft) lengths of wool. (Shorter lengths are easier to handle when wrapping the wool around the cardboard.)

3

Sandwich the cardboard rings together. Thread a length of wool through the needle and start winding the wool around the ring, moving evenly and slowly covering the cardboard. Just before each length of wool is finished, tie on the next length and continue winding until the hole in the ring is full with wool.

4

Carefully insert scissors between the cardboard rings and begin to cut through the wool. Cut all the way around the circle.

5

Thread a 20 cm (8 in) length of wool around the middle of the cardboard rings and firmly tie a knot to secure the pompom strands. Repeat with another 20 cm (8 in) length of wool, tying the knot on the opposite side of the pompom. Trim these lengths of wool to around 8 cm (3 in). (There should be 2 strands hanging from the top and 2 from the bottom of the pompom. The bottom 2 will become the legs and the top 2 can be used to tie the pompom to gifts.) Slide the cardboard rings off the wool.

6

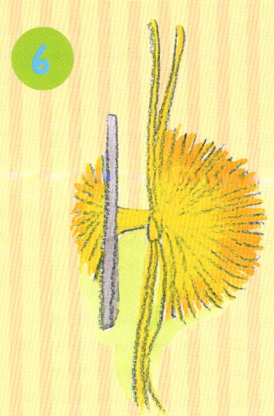

Fluff and shape the wool into a pompom ball. Trim away any knots and odd strands of wool, being careful not to cut off the legs or top strands.

7

Trace the beak, feet and comb templates on page 46 onto tracing paper. Cut out the tracing paper shapes.

8

Cut out 2 beak triangles in orange felt by holding the tracing paper template over the felt and cutting around it. Insert into the pompom above the legs, with the triangles facing each other to form an open beak. Glue into position.

9

Cut out 4 feet from black felt using the tracing paper template. Glue 2 feet together at the ends of each leg.

10

Cut out a comb in red felt using the tracing paper templates. Glue the eyes into position above the beak and glue the comb at the top of the head.

Daffodil
(page 20)

Pompom chick
(page 44)

Beak x 2

Comb

Feet x 4

Egg card
(page 36)

Cardboard ring

Poppy
(page 38)

Paper egg
(page 12)

Zigzag shape
(page 12)

Bunny mask
(page 10)
Photocopy at 130% to enlarge

Cut 2 sets of inner ears

Cut along line, overlap and staple

Cut 1 nose